The Black Ca
Made Me Buy It!

written and designed by

ALICE L. MUNCASTER & ELLEN SAWYER

Photography by Peter Basdeka

CROWN PUBLISHERS, INC.
New York

This book is dedicated to
all the cats we have loved,
even the ones that weren't black.

Published by Crown Publishers, Inc., 225 Park Avenue South, New York, New York 10003,
and represented in Canada by the Canadian MANDA Group

CROWN is a trademark of Crown Publishers, Inc.

Manufactured in Hong Kong

Library of Congress Cataloging-in-Publication Data
Muncaster, Alice L.
The black cat made me buy it!

1. Cats in advertising—Collectors and collecting.
2. Americana—Collectors and collecting.
I. Sawyer, Ellen II. Title
HF5827.M85 1988   659.1′96368′009   87–37972
ISBN 0–517–56891–8

10 9 8 7 6 5 4 3 2 1

First Edition

Introduction

If a black cat crosses your path, what's your reaction? Are you a person who believes bad luck will surely follow or do you merely smile at such nonsense?

Black cats were once thought to have mystical powers, but today cat enthusiasts know that the only power these beautiful creatures have is the ability to evoke strong emotions from humans.

People seem either to *love* black cats or they have an aversion to them. Such opposite reactions are the result of centuries of controversy. But the controversy, and the superstitions that fueled its growth, left the black cat with a reputation it never deserved.

Centuries ago, black cats were considered symbols of good luck almost as often as they were seen as bad omens. Unfortunately for the cats, there were no telephones or televisions, so this kind of news didn't travel fast. But bad

luck stories, just like bad gossip, always managed to get around. So the bad luck reputation prevailed.

You've probably guessed by now that we are not impartial observers of the black cats' situation. As animal lovers, we never believed that black cats were different from other kinds of cats. Then, as we collected antiques featuring cat motifs, we began to see that black cats appeared quite often in a wide variety of artistic and decorative applications.

Of particular importance was our discovery that black cats appeared in a great deal of advertising over the past hundred years or so. Consider this: if black cats truly were perceived as harbingers of disaster, why would so many manufacturers and retailers have selected the Black Cat brand name or used a black cat as the attention-getting device in advertising for their products? Wouldn't superstition and fear drive consumers away

Postcards were the most popular form of correspondence in the first decades of this century. Louis Wain, who created these charming kittens at the seashore, was well known for his drawings of cats. This card was one of a series from the early 1900s, when comic animal scenes—first popular in Victorian times—were still much in demand.

from buying items that carried the Black Cat name—items like Black Cat coffee, hosiery, cigarettes, matches, ribbon, and whiskey?

The answer is no. Black Cat brands and advertising that pictured black cats proliferated and, by far, black cats have been the kind of cat most often shown in product ads, particularly during the Victorian era.

In somewhat the same kind of puzzle, if people were really afraid of black cats, would they want black cat images displayed in their homes as decorations? Of course not! It was our pleasure to find many beautiful examples of black cats used in the decorative arts from folk paintings to high-tech interior design.

So, if actions speak louder than words, there is good evidence that black cats really have not been seriously viewed as fearsome creatures— at least during the eighteenth to twentieth centuries. And today, the black cat is one of America's most popular pets!

The bad luck angle seems to have had its roots in the folk history of many nations. Much of it was never written down but was passed from generation to generation by stories and songs.

As people from other countries emigrated to America, their traditions came with them. And, although good luck stories were nearly as numerous in folk tales as bad luck versions, it was just bad luck for black cats that more people came to America from countries where bad luck stories were carefully remembered and retold.

Above left: When celebrations call for fireworks, Black Cat® firecrackers can often be found at the scene. Li & Fung (Trading) Limited of Hong Kong introduced the Black Cat brand in 1952. The company is known for improving the quality and safety of fireworks by replacing mud seals on firecrackers with paper seals. This soon became the industry standard. Originally an exporting firm, Li & Fung was founded in 1906 and today has diversified business interests including electronics, textiles, and retail stores.

Left: This smiling black cat was one of a series of modern postcards offered by the Taylor & Ng company, Oakland, California, in the 1970s.

The references to black cats as demons, witches, or companions of the devil were documented in the Middle Ages, where primitive living conditions, poor nutrition, lack of sanitation, and rampant disease all contributed to short life expectancies for everyone. A black cat could be blamed for death just because it entered the room of a dying person. And if another member of the family became ill (with what we now know was a contagious disease), the poor cat was likely to be blamed again!

During the famous witch trials in the 1600s, some people who were accused of being witches were piteously tortured until they admitted all sorts of things—and a few either had black cats as pets or admitted being acquainted with one! These "confessions" were bad for black cats because "witches" were supposedly the accomplices of Satan—and religious people were likely to believe that the cats were, too.

Since religion was an important influence in Europe, and the black cat/evil omen superstition had religious overtones, emigrants to America brought their fearful stories to the New World. In fact, the belief that bad luck will befall you if a black cat crosses your path comes from an early European superstition that a black cat walking across your path is marking a path to Satan. And no matter what other differences the various religious sects of Europe had, they were all unified in their teachings against the devil.

Historians would point out that folk traditions should not be dismissed as nonsense.

A traditional arched-back cat ready to defend its turf helped dramatize the name of Honest Scrap chewing tobacco around the turn of the century. This cardboard easel-backed advertising sign stood on countertops in tobacco shops and general stores. It is unusual because it only shows the cat. Most Honest Scrap advertising also pictured a dog preparing to "scrap" with its feline rival. When this brand was popular, Americans preferred chewing tobacco to smoking cigarettes, cigars, or pipes.

5

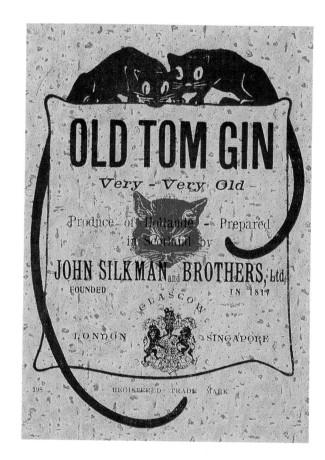

Black cats brought good luck (and sales success) to the makers of Lucky Cat incense powder. The brand was available for forty-five years after it was first introduced in 1939. This package is from the late 1960s. A companion product, Black Cat Candles, was also introduced in 1939 and was sold through the 1960s.

These cute, stylized black cats looked eager to go home with buyers of this brand of "Old Tom" gin. "Old Tom" was the generic name for a type of sweetened gin that was popular in Victorian times but has all but disappeared since the end of World War II. It was especially popular for use in hot gin toddies.

They acknowledge that references to cats and spiritualism are found in records of civilizations that lived centuries before the birth of Christ. The ancient Egyptians believed that cats guided souls to the hereafter. Bastet (or Pasht), the cat goddess, was also considered the goddess of light. In Oriental cultures, cats were considered reincarnated human souls.

But these associations with spiritualism were not considered evil, as strange as they seem. It was only later, when different cultural philosophies prevailed, that any such association with spirits began to cause trouble for cats—and black cats in particular.

With education and enlightenment, things changed. People now realize that black cats have been the victims of some sad misunderstandings in the past. But they also realize that while people in one country or region or state were telling bad luck black cat stories, other people were passing along good luck tales about black cats.

The photographs in this book show black cats in some of their traditional and non-traditional roles. You'll see some Halloween cats, but you'll notice that many artists portrayed the typical arched-back cat in cute and nonthreatening ways, while still acknowledging the witches-and-goblin theme of the holiday. You'll see black cats in advertising, both as the endorsers of some products and as the symbol or brand name of others. There are some mysterious black cats. Many decorative goods show black cats as favorite pets or stylized images. And you'll see a number of examples of good luck black cats!

The Black Cat

November, 1896.

Silas F. Quigley — To Arrive.
Lewis Hopkins Rogers.

The Polar Magnet.
Philip Verrill Mighels.

Fitzhugh.
W. Macpherson Wiltbank.

The Passionate Snake.
Ella Higginson.

Professor Whirlwind.
Allen Quinan.

5 CENTS

THE SHORTSTORY PUBLISHING CO. 144 HIGH ST., BOSTON, MASS.

The Black Cat was a fiction magazine of the late nineteenth century and early twentieth century. See pages 74–75 for more about this unusual publication.

HARPER'S
WEEKLY

EDITED BY GEORGE HARVEY

December 18 1909   HARPER & BROTHERS, N.Y.   Price 10 Cents

Black Cats and Halloween

lack cats have often been stereotyped as "Halloween" cats. The familiar arched-back, hissing cat has been a standard image on cards, decorations, and costumes for the popular October occasion.

The roots of this reason, of course, lie in the association people made in the past between witches and cats, as well as the naturally mysterious image of the black cat itself.

But, as you will see on the following pages, black cats have made the best of their bad publicity through the twentieth century. And black cats have been defended by countless artists as they illustrated cards and magazine covers, designed unique party decorations, and made trick-or-treat accessories.

Some of their work can be found here—easily identified by the type of black cat they created. These are cute and happy-looking black cats—not the devil's accomplices! They add some fun to the Halloween holiday. They entertain rather than frighten.

These cats are important symbols of the black cat's progress toward being accepted as a normal pet. America is aging. The early immigrants from countries where superstition governed daily activity are gone, and their descendants are viewing the ways of the old country as simple folk customs, not doctrine. People look to science for explanations of the complex matters of life and death. The old tales of superstition are just not very important in today's advanced world.

Children still see plenty of black cat images around Halloween, but for the most part the cats are purely decorative instead of scary. With the growing popularity of cats as pets, more homes today have black cats around than ever before. So children can see firsthand that there's no truth to any lingering black cat/bad luck superstitions, no matter what time of the year it is!

These Halloween seals are as desirable today as they were when they were sold by The Dennison Company in the 1920s. Dennison Halloween costumes and party decorations were always popular because the designs were particularly creative and appealing.

A fluffy, friendly black kitten and a youngster in a witch costume were typical of the Halloween illustrations found on October magazine covers in the early 1900s. But this one appeared in December! *Harper's Weekly* was a well-respected newsmagazine founded in 1857 by the Harper & Brothers publishing house of New York City. It was best known for its timely woodcut engravings of important news events, particularly the Civil War, and for its political influence. The last issue was published in 1916.

These deeply embossed cardboard cats are typical Halloween party decorations of yesteryear. The arched-back cat was made in Germany and measures 10½″ tall; the companion face was 7½″ tall. Both are the kind that were popular in the 1920s and 1930s.

Halloween lanterns were popular decorations in the 1920–1950 era. The shaped papier-mâché cat from the early 1920s is 5″ tall and has green paper eyes that glow when a candle is lit inside. The 6″-tall rectangular lantern is made of cardboard and transparent tissue paper. It was made by The Beistle Company from 1942 through 1962. Martin Luther Beistle started making artificial flowers in his basement workshop in 1900 and in the early 1920s diversified into party goods and seasonal decorations. Over 2,000 such items are now offered by The Beistle Company.

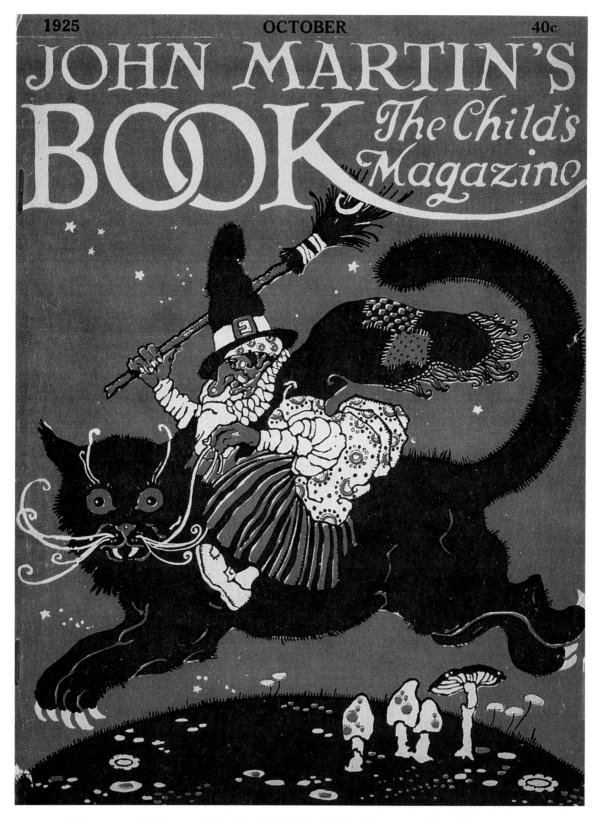

JOHN MARTIN'S BOOK *The Child's Magazine*

The cover of *John Martin's Book* undoubtedly delighted young readers when it was published in 1925. The children who received this monthly magazine probably never knew that there was a historical connection between this whimsical cat and witch and the tales of witches riding animals through the sky that prevailed during the Middle Ages. *John Martin's Book* contained stories and activity guides for children.

A smiling "trick-or-treat" cat made this an exceptionally appealing Halloween card offered by Drawing Board Greeting Cards in 1985 and 1986. Barbara Kingery, a Drawing Board staff artist, created the cat. The company was founded in 1956 and produces cards, gift wrap, stationery, and calendars.

"Halloween cats" are all different—they are as diverse as the artists and craftsmen who create them. The mask at the right is over fifty years old and is particularly detailed for a paper creation. The sleek lines of Art Deco design can be seen in the cast-iron and glass candy dish from the late 1920s or early 1930s. Both items were undoubtedly enjoyed at numerous Halloween parties through the years before they found their way into private collections.

Noisemakers have remained part of the Halloween tradition through the years even though we no longer believe in the spirits and spooks such devices were supposed to scare away. The 6″-tall tin bell is from the 1930s and has a black cat and a broom-riding witch alternately lithographed on its sides. The 1940s die-cut (shaped) cardboard and cloth cat is 5″ tall and squeaks loudly when squeezed.

Sending Halloween cards is still part of the fun of celebrating Halloween, some seventy years after these postcards were made. Many old cards like these depict cats and other symbols of Halloween as cute and friendly rather than fierce and scary—a tradition continued today by greeting card manufacturers. The "Hallowe'en Pleasures" card was printed by Whitney in Worcester, Massachusetts; "A Happy Hallowe'en" is from the Henderson Litho Company, Cincinnati, Ohio.

The three figural cats at the left are candy containers. The largest is mohair-covered papier-mâché from the turn of the century and stands 6″ tall. The head lifts off to reveal a hollow body where the candy was stored. Both of the others are glazed papier-mâché. The pumpkin cat has a fabric tail and originally sold for fifteen cents at an Oklahoma City variety store (the tag is still affixed). Halloween novelties like these were popular in the 1940s and 1950s.

Designers of Halloween decorations have always been faced with the challenge of creating new designs to differentiate their work from the competition. The Beistle Company came up with the unusual "electric" black cat cardboard decorations shown here. The largest of the arched-back die-cuts measured 11″ tall; the smallest, just 4½″. They were packaged with the more traditional witch-and-cat cutouts. "Beistle makes them by the million" was the company's slogan in the 1930s when decorations and other party goods for every occasion were displayed for prospective buyers both at their Pennsylvania factory and at a showroom on Fifth Avenue in New York City. Today the company is the largest U.S. manufacturer of seasonal decorations and party goods.

Black Cats in Advertising

It's easy to see that black cats are quite prominent in advertising. Actually, *all* kinds of cats have been found in advertising over the past 100 years, as seen in our previous two books, but black cats seem to be the favorite choice to represent many products.

Because of the legends and superstitions that surrounded black cats many years ago, black cats naturally drew considerable attention to themselves wherever they appeared. That meant they could also draw attention to any product they posed with or were intended to represent. While clever marketers extended the cat's use in advertising by linking the qualities of a cat to their product—such as softness, sleekness, beauty, or surefootedness—the use of black cats went a step further to also add mystery and intrigue.

Another reason they were so popular was purely economic. Before printing technology advanced to modern capabilities, simple printing presses could only accommodate one ink color at a time. The one that was easiest to read was used most often—and that was black. Each additional color increased the cost of the printing job, so most advertisers just used black ink. This meant that sometimes cats were colored black in advertising solely as a cost-cutting measure, not because they had any particular meaning!

Even when cost was not a deciding factor, black cats appeared in an amazing number of advertisements. When you look at the black cats shown in this section, you can see that, in some cases, almost any color of cat could have been substituted. But they weren't. Black cats were undoubtedly selected for their universal appeal and attention-getting qualities.

Or maybe they were just lucky!

The black cat has appeared over the years on hundreds of matchbox labels in many different countries. The examples here show that the black cat theme was universal in the early years of this century—in places as diverse as Belgium, Japan, and the Philippines.

A black cat was the unusual but instantly recognizable product symbol for the L. H. Thomas Co. of Chicago (1885–1931). The company made inks and household paste. This 20″-tall in-store promotional statue is made of papier-mâché and has golden glass eyes.

"WHAT SHALL I WRITE TO MARIA?"
"PULL MY EAR AND SEE."

The Thomas' Ink cat was found on bottles of the company's ink and on its jars of paste and mucilage. No one is sure how the cat became the corporate symbol, but its use made the product stand out on store shelves as "the one with the cat on the label." The Thomas Co. produced several kinds of writing fluids, and the products consistently won the highest awards in competitions at fairs and expositions, including the 1885 New Orleans Exposition and the World's Columbian Exposition held in Chicago in 1893.

The package shown at the left is made of lithographed tin. It originally held a small corked bottle of ink and a marking pad. When empty, it could also serve as an inkwell. It is only 3¼" x 2" and dates to the late 1800s. The writing cat, above left, is a "mechanical" die-cut advertising card from the same time period. When the cat's ear is pulled, the tablet of paper in front of the cat slides away to show the message—"Use Thomas' Inks." It measures 5½" x 4".

The beautiful lithographed tin sign at the right features a realistic-looking black cat getting into mischief—in Thomas' Ink, of course. The Writing Fluid No. 9 was promoted for bookkeeping and record keeping use because it "writes a bright blue, changes to an everlasting black." The Sanford Corporation long ago acquired the L. H. Thomas Co., but the products with the cat on the bottle are no longer made.

21

During the 1880–1930 era, cigars were more popular than cigarettes in the United States. Cigar box labels were sold by lithographers to thousands of cigar manufacturers and sellers across the country—either already printed with a design they kept in stock, or customized for an extra cost. The Night Clerk brand (ca. 1900–1910) was offered by the Imperial Cigar Co. Cigar bands were wrapped around the cigars so, even if sold singly, the brand was identifiable. The unnamed black cat band is an example of a "stock art" design—one that could have been used by any number of cigar makers or sellers.

When the United States entered World War I in 1917, the U.S. Tank Corps featured a huge black cat drawn by artist Angiet Hutaf in its recruiting materials. The window card shown at the right measures 9¾″ x 14″. The cat also helped recruit soldiers on full-size posters.

A clever visual word play explains the presence of a cat on the label above that advertises a modern German pain-killing tablet. Vivimed claims to be the remedy for headaches, toothaches, and even a hangover. *"Kater"* means both "hangover" and "cat," depending on how the word is used! The French labels below appeared on contemporary Gourmet Cat brand cheeses. The song shown on the label describes a purring feline sampling the company's product.

The menu and wine list on the opposite page is a striking example of Art Deco design. Patrons of the Kit Kat Cabaret in Montreal, Quebec, had the pleasure of ordering lobster Newburg for $1.50 and spaghetti for 75 cents during the 1930s, when this supper menu was printed. Today, office buildings tower over the site of the once prosperous cabaret.

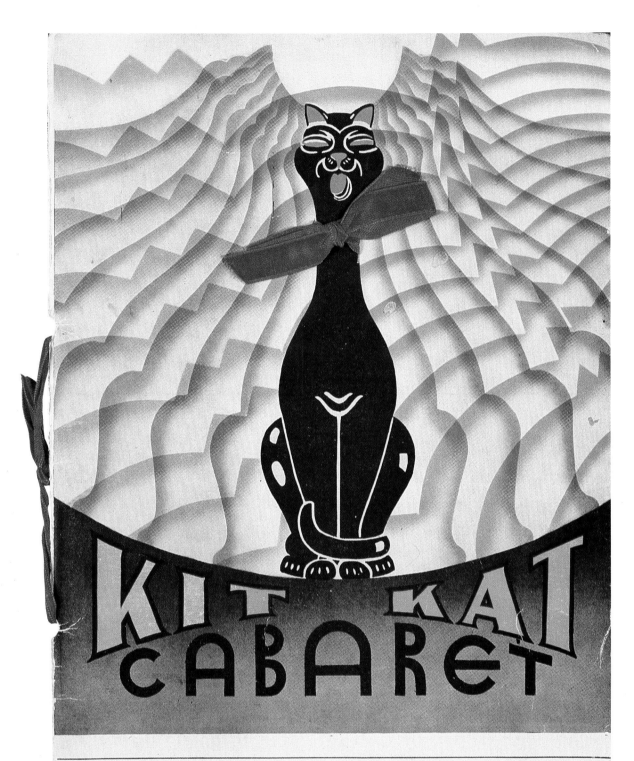

KIT KAT CABARET

COUVERT   CHARGE $1.00   per   Person

SATURDAY & HOLIDAYS $1.50 per Person

SHOWS:
at 11.30 P.M.
and 1.45 A.M.

This cardboard cat face was given away as a promotional tactic by the James Van Dyk Co., a retail coffee and tea business in New York. There was a space on the back for recording the height and weight of a child. Employees probably weighed customers' children right in the store and sent the proud parents home with the cat premium as a goodwill gesture. Of course, the company's advertising message was also printed on the back. The Van Dyk company claimed to open a new branch store every month and already had fifty locations at the time this promotion took place around 1900.

Both the Van Dyk company's die-cut cat and the cigar label shown below are examples of art produced by printing firms in the late 1800s and early 1900s. Designs were commissioned by the printers and sold to product manufacturers and stores, customized for different uses. Gordon's Cats was most likely a custom brand label made for a small cigar factory or a tobacco shop.

THE MODERN WITCH* weaves a spell
in fine, full-fashioned hosiery

THE Modern Witch of Ipswich has woven a potent hosiery charm in a new full-fashioned hose of pure thread silk.

It has a truly bewitching perfection of weave and perfection of fit. Its fine, even texture will remind you of imported French hosiery, for it has been fashioned on specially-made imported machines.

No small part of this hosiery charm is the sleek perfection of fit—shaped in snugly at the ankle and instep, with an extra fullness at the calf and at the garter hem and, most important of all, an extra length of silk above the knee. The reinforced garter hem and slipper sole insure long wear. In all the smartest shades now being worn in Paris.

And remember, back of the Modern Witch is the century-old Ipswich secret of unrivalled durability and exceptional value that distinguishes all Ipswich hosiery.

*A witch, according to the dictionary, is one who "exerts power more than natural; an irresistible influence." In this sense Ipswich is truly "The Modern Witch" of hosiery, for Ipswich sets the standard for beauty, fineness and durability in smart hosiery.

IPSWICH HOSIERY

IPSWICH MILLS, Ipswich, Mass.   LAWRENCE & CO., Sole Selling Agents

The Modern Witch

The Ipswich Mills trademark of a broom-riding witch came to life in the 1927 magazine advertisement shown above. The bewitching costumed "flapper" girl and her pet cast a creepy witch-and-Halloween-cat shadow to play upon the Ipswich name. Unfortunately, the company was too late in its attempt to capture a share of the "full-fashioned" hosiery market. Changing styles in women's clothing in the mid-1920s created a huge demand for snug-fitting new-fashioned hosiery—but Ipswich specialized in the old-fashioned circular-knitted kind that women had worn since the early 1800s. Although Ipswich had grown to a large operation with mills in four New England towns, the company went out of business in 1928. Ipswich equipment was sold to a group of Russian businessmen who set up a hosiery-making factory near Moscow.

Stop in at almost any shoe repair shop across America today, and you'll see the familiar Cat's Paw black cat symbol. The cat has been in this business since the Cat's Paw brand name was first used in the early 1900s.

The celluloid pins below were early promotional items given away to customers by dealers of Cat's Paw products. The full-bodied black cat was the symbol used throughout the first few decades of this century. Then, in 1941, the more modern version of the logo was drawn for the Cat's Paw Rubber Company by Lucien Bernhard.

The cat has always figured prominently in Cat's Paw advertising, including its use on boxes and window decals, such as those shown on the opposite page. "Blackie," the character shown in the advertisement at the left, was used by the company in comic strip–style magazine ads in the 1950s.

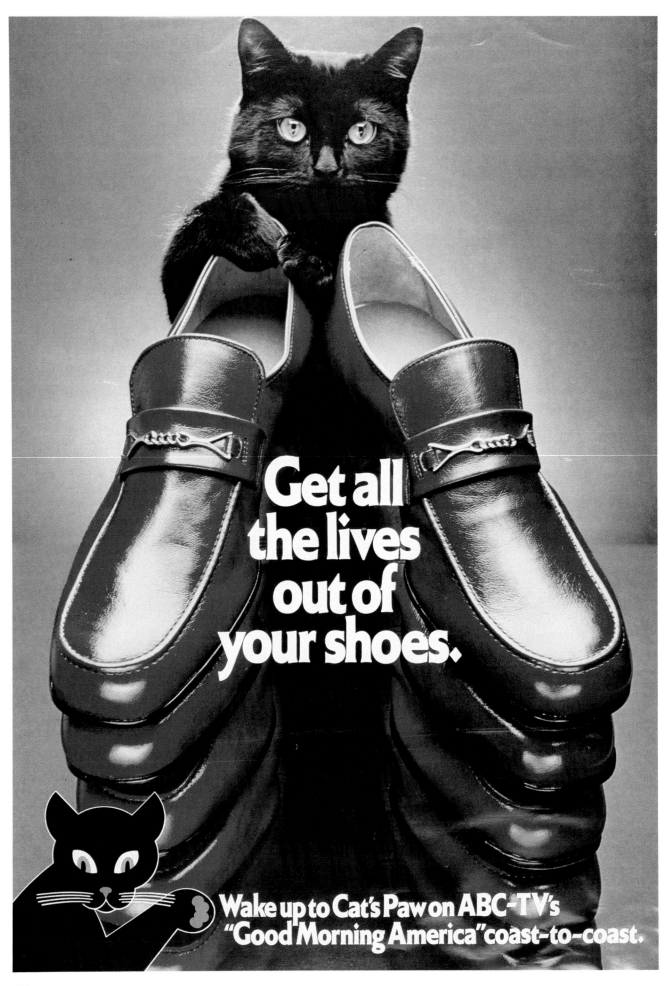

Get all
the lives
out of
your shoes.

Wake up to Cat's Paw on ABC-TV's
"Good Morning America" coast-to-coast.

The majority of early cigar makers in America long ago ceased operations or were bought out by large tobacco conglomerates. By some estimates, there were at one time hundreds of thousands of small cigar factories in the United States, because even small towns often had a local cigar-making operation when cigars were the fashionable smoke. The names "Two Toms" and "Wizard" appear in listings of tobacco brands from several companies around the turn of the century. The gold-tone embossing was a process used in the late 1800s and early 1900s.

The Cat's Paw symbol was depicted as a real cat in the 1985 advertising poster shown at the left. Photography is used more often than original art in most kinds of advertising of the 1980s.

This booklet was a log book for amateur radio enthusiasts produced as an advertising premium by Katz Drug Stores. It was no coincidence that Katz had a cat as the company's symbol. Ike Katz and his brother Mike capitalized on their sound-alike surname and put little cat's heads on their advertising and private-label merchandise to help people remember their name. The brothers started out with a fruit stand in Kansas City, Missouri, expanded to a confectionery store and then a cigar store, and they added a line of pharmaceuticals in 1914 because only drugstores were allowed extended hours of operation during World War I.

Katz expanded on the more volume/less profit theory to become a leader in the cut-rate retail drug business. With brilliant public relations and promotional tactics—from the famous "Katz pays the tax" tobacco promotion during World War I to huge public parties and concerts through the 1950s and 1960s—Katz became a huge chain of stores in the Midwest and South. Katz stores were acquired in 1971 by Skaggs Companies, Inc., another large discount drugstore chain, now owned by American Stores Company.

Brightener and Old English polishes helped make the A. S. Boyle Company of Cincinnati, Ohio, a leading household products firm in the early 1900s. Here, a black cat demonstrated that floors polished with Brightener really shine. This ad appeared on the back cover of *The Burr McIntosh Monthly Magazine* in April 1909.

Brightener

Keeps Floors
Bright and Clean
All the Time

Just apply a cloth moistened with a little "**Brightener**"—no more work than dusting. It cleans the floor and brightens the finish. If you do this once in two or three weeks it keeps your floors like new all the time. A quart (for 75c) will last the average home six months. If you have never used "**Brightener**"

SEND FOR FREE SAMPLE

And try it. You will be glad to know of it. "**Brightener**" is the only preparation that will successfully clean and polish a waxed floor without removing the wax, or a varnished floor without injuring the finish. As a matter of fact, it makes wax or varnish last twice as long. Never use water or oil preparations—they ruin the finish. Study how to make your floors beautiful and you will discover that the appearance of the floor determines largely the aesthetic effect of the room.

Write for our free Book "Beautiful Floors—their Finish and Care."

It is a book for study and reference and contains expert advice in plain terms on such subjects as

Woods Fit for Flooring	Stopping Cracks in Floors
Care of Waxed Floors	Finishing Kitchen, Pantry, Bath Room Floors
Cleaning and Polishing Hardwood Floors	Finishing Dance Floors
Finishing New Floors	Finishing Furniture and Interior Woodwork
Finishing Old Floors	Removing Varnish, Shellac and Paint

Please mention your paint dealer's name when you write for the free sample of "**Brightener**" and the book. If he doesn't get "**Brightener**" when you want it you may order it from us (after you try the sample) 40c pint; 75c quart; $2.50 gallon.

A. S. BOYLE & CO., 1900 West 8th St., Cincinnati, Ohio

Manufacturers of "THE WAX WITH A GUARANTEE"—

Old English Floor Wax

World Renowned for its "QUALITY."

This wall-hanging match holder was given away around 1900 to customers of The Outlet, one of the best-known and most respected retail operations in New England. Joseph and Leon Samuels started a small discount clothing store in 1884 and guided its growth into a retail giant through smart pricing and clever sales promotion.

The Outlet was known for its colorful events through the years—including everything from lavish parades to even bringing elephants into the store for customers to pet! After growing to 158 stores in the Eastern United States, The Outlet company sold its merchandising operations to another retail chain in 1980 and concentrated on its broadcasting division established in 1922. Today, Outlet Communications owns radio and television stations across America.

This large-sized label (9⅞″ x 17½″) is the kind affixed to wooden crates of goods shipped to stores in the late nineteenth and early twentieth centuries—before cardboard boxes made it possible to print directly on the box. The same black cat and its rival appeared on many other Vulcan labels and packages in a wide variety of sizes.

34

This die-cut stand-up advertising sign helped Julius Maggi sell his powdered soup invention in Europe around the turn of the century. Maggi worked closely with Swiss officials to develop the product, designed to save time in the kitchen so working mothers could still cook nutritious meals for their families. The first Maggi soups were introduced in 1884 and the company joined Nestlé S.A. in 1947. Maggi soups continue to be a leading brand in Europe today.

This smiling black cat is an 1896 die-cut promotional piece sent to customers of Dunham, Buckley & Co. of New York City. It was mailed in its own envelope that carried an obvious play on words, so the recipient had to bring the cat out of the "bag" to read the advertising message printed on the back of the cat. Drap moscovietta was a kind of corded dress fabric popular in Victorian times.

A cat was considered the natural symbol to represent Gatto Gelato, a specialty dessert shop that served fresh Italian-style flavored ices and frozen cremes in Chicago from 1984 to 1986. After all, cats are known to love cream! But a black cat silhouette was selected because it could represent all kinds of cats, not just one particular breed. Officials of ARA Services, owners of the shop, said the "generic" cat also represented the many different kinds of people who love ice-cream treats. As ARA developed the logo, they visualized a cat silently slipping off to the kitchen in search of a bowl of fresh cream—much as workers in the ninety-five-story Chicago skyscraper where Gatto Gelato was located might slip off for an undetected frozen dessert in the shop's secluded location in the building.

A stylized black cat designed by New York artist Clarence Cole has been featured on Eveready carbon zinc batteries since 1948. Union Carbide Company officials adopted the symbol of a cat dashing through the numeral 9 to illustrate that their batteries, like the proverbial cat, have nine lives. The symbolism was considered appropriate because carbon zinc batteries drop in voltage as they are used, but then bounce right back after a period of rest, like a playful cat after a nap! The in-store display shown above was part of a 1982 promotion to stimulate battery sales. The plastic cat bank was offered free when designated proofs of purchase from battery packages were mailed to the company.

"Tom," the Mr. Thomas cigars symbol, could be found on promotional items such as the lithographed tin change tray shown above and the advertising postcard below. The Ruhe Brothers company knew the value of creating a strong brand identification symbol, and consistently used the cat to promote recognition of their product. The change tray is 4¼" in diameter and was given to owners of tobacco shops or general stores around the turn of the century. When a sale was registered, it was customary for the store owner to put the customer's change in the tray—of course, the customer saw the advertising message when the change was picked up.

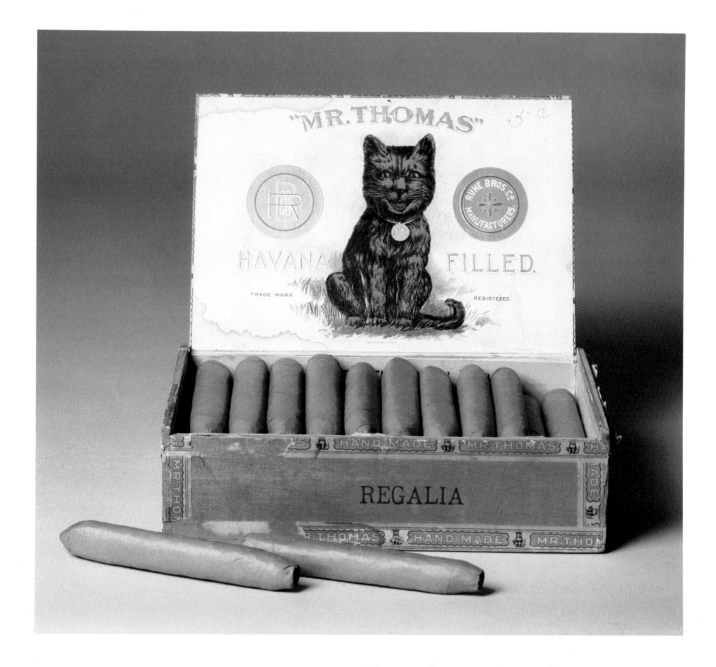

This Mr. Thomas wooden cigar box was made between 1910 and 1916. The Ruhe Brothers company made sure "Tom" was on the inner lid label and stamped onto the outside top of the box, too. The Mr. Thomas name and tiny black cats were also used on the edge trim on the box. Such edging was used not only to cover up the muslin cloth hinge that held the box top and bottom together, but also all around the box to reinforce the brand identity.

Cuban cigars have always been known for their fine tobacco, and American companies that used Cuban tobacco in the late 1800s and early 1900s often emphasized this fact by putting Spanish words on their boxes (such as "Regalia") and mentioning Havana whenever possible (as on the paper liner wording: "Havana Filled"). Mr. Thomas cigar bands featured the cat, too, so that individual cigars were easily identified even when they were no longer in the box. The size of box shown above held fifty cigars.

Many companies not only used black cats in advertising but also named products after the cats. By far, the most popular of these names is "Black Cat."

Black Cat brands shown on the following pages date back to the late 1800s. They seem to have been most widely used in Victorian times, but many can still be found on store shelves today.

Since black cats are found in the folk legends and traditions of many countries, it is understandable that black cats would be pictured on packages and labels in European and Asian countries as well as in America. In countries where the black cat always represented good luck, this symbol on the package might have subliminally linked good luck with the purchase of the product. Even in countries where good luck and black cats seemed to be opposite themes, superstition was often ignored when it came to naming products! The attention these cats commanded more than made up for any old-fashioned ideas that black cats brought bad luck.

It was in America, where many nationalities were blended, that the Black Cat brand was most often found—on both domestic and imported goods. Although most of these products are no longer sold, we can appreciate their heritage and beautiful design even today.

Black Cat London Dry Gin was sold from Victorian times through the 1960s by the James Burroughs company of England. This label (enlarged) is from the 1920s. Cats and gin products have been associated for hundreds of years in Europe, where one kind of sweetened gin even bears the generic title of "Old Tom" gin. One legend says that a London distiller created a type of coin-operated gin-vending machine in the shape of a black cat as far back as the 1700s!

Advertising on matchboxes was—and still is—an easy way to promote products. Every time a cigarette or pipe was lit in pre-cigarette lighter days, a matchbox label put the product name at a consumer's fingertips. These French labels (enlarged) advertised Black Cat Coffee.

The extremely colorful label for Black Cat Apples below shows that the use of a black cat symbol is universal. The label was the kind used on fruit crates shipped from grower to seller in the 1920s and 1930s. The Black Cat brand was produced by the International Fruit and Mercantile Co., Victoria, Australia.

The Black Cat Hosiery Company was one of the most visible advertisers of the late 1890s and early 1900s. The Cooper brothers—Charles, Willis, and Henry—started the company in Kenosha, Wisconsin, and gained nationwide recognition for the Black Cat brand through imaginative magazine advertising. The story booklet shown below was given to children in an 1899 Christmas promotion. Of course, advertising information was woven into the story! The Coopers also operated the Cooper Underwear Company and manufactured underwear under the White Cat brand—using the same cat trademark as they created for their hosiery, but in white. Two of the Coopers died in a tragic theater fire in Chicago in 1903, and the hosiery business was sold in 1913. The underwear company thrived and in 1971 became Jockey International, Inc.

The magazine ads on the opposite page show the creativity of Black Cat stockings ads from 1899 *(top)*, 1902 *(center)*, and 1898 *(bottom)*.

To draw attention to the Black Cat brand, this 22″-high three-dimensional trademark could be placed in a store window or on a countertop. The cat is made of lithographed cardboard and could also be hung on a wall.

BLACK CAT BRAND HOSIERY BLACK CAT BRAND

Black Cat Colorado Claro cigars were made in Iowa before 1910. The words "Colorado Claro" told the buyer that the cigars were mild, designating that they were made from the second-lightest–colored tobacco available. The cat face on the label is very similar to the cat face used on *The Black Cat* magazines shown on pages 7 and 75 and the game spinner shown on page 87, but there does not appear to be any connection among the items.

Zeller Schwarze Katz is one of the best-known types of white wine exported from Germany. Legend has it that visiting wine merchants proclaimed wine from the barrel on which a black cat was sitting as the best entry at a turn-of-the-century German wine tasting. Ever since, this particular type of white wine has been known as the Black Cat wine—Zeller Schwarze Katz.

Zeller Schwarze Katz is a full, elegant, and fruity white wine, made from grapes grown in the tiny Zell an der Mosel region of Germany.

Shown at the left are wine bottles from the 1970s for different brands of Zeller Schwarze Katz: Leonard Kreusch Wines, Inc.; Julius Kayser & Co.; and Tytell (Canandaigua Wine Co., Inc.). The promotional tin shown here was offered in the mid-1980s by Julius Kayser & Co. Three bottles of wine were packed inside. The happy-faced Kayser cat also appears on the cover of this book.

The adorable plushy black cat shown above is a 1987 promotional device created by Julius Kayser & Co. The Zeller Schwarze Katz symbol measures 13″ tall and was designed to sit high atop a retail store display of Kayser Zeller Schwarze Katz wine. When properly positioned, the cat would be about six to seven feet in the air. It would be easy to spot from just about anywhere in the store and would automatically remind shoppers of the Black Cat brand.

The souvenir program booklet at the right is from Le Chat Noir (The Black Cat), a famous Paris cabaret frequented by artists and political liberals in the late 1800s and early 1900s. Théophile Steinlen, well known for his many paintings and drawings of cats, was a regular visitor there. This booklet is from around 1915, when the establishment had moved from its original location and was under new management. Although the cat on the cover looks similar in style to those drawn by Steinlen, it is not the creation of the famous artist.

Programme Souvenir

CHAT-NOIR

THE BLACK CAT

68
Boulevard
de
Clichy

Paris-Montmartre

« Quo non ascendam ? »

CABARET

ARTISTIQUE

Direction : Jehan Chagot

One of the most interesting black cat brands is Black Cat tobacco and cigarettes from England. The company has a long history, dating back to a small tobacconist's shop in London in the 1840s. Here, it is said, a black cat roamed freely, and it became such a familiar sight sleeping in the window that the shop became known as The Black Cat Shop. The Carreras family, owners of the shop, catered to European nobility with their custom blends of cut tobacco. In 1886, the Black Cat brand was registered by the Carreras company.

In 1904, Black Cat cigarettes were introduced—one of the first machine-made brands sold in England. During World War II, Black Cat cigarettes, like many other brands, were withdrawn from the market and were not reintroduced until 1957. In 1959, a filtered version replaced the earlier unfiltered kind but today, the famous Black Cat brand is no longer available. The celluloid-topped match holder shown below (enlarged) is a "match safe" made around 1915. Pocket match safes were popular in the late 1800s and early 1900s. Advertisers often put their messages on a celluloid surface attached to the top or side of the safe. This charming Black Cat item measures 2⅜″ x 1⅞″, but was enlarged here to show the cats' antics in the advertising illustration.

The black cat symbol always appeared on Black Cat brand tobacco packaging. The variety of cigarette packages *(top right)* shows the different Black Cat designs used over the years. The company heavily promoted the brand, and the Black Cat album *(bottom right)* was one of the company's earliest promotional items given free to customers. Collectible stamps were included in packs of the cigarettes and were supposed to be pasted in the album. Prizes were given for completed albums, encouraging brand loyalty. The pretty die-cut black cat is an easel-backed display used at stores and shops where Black Cat cigarettes were sold.

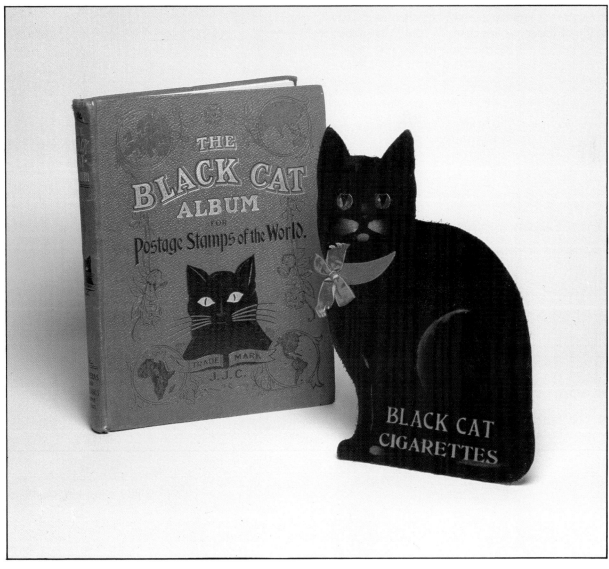

Originally, the Black Cat trademark only represented Carreras cut tobacco. The pocket tin at the right predates the cigarettes' 1904 introduction. The J.J.C. under the cat stands for Jose Joaquin Carreras, son of the founder of the Carreras company and the proprietor of the original Black Cat tobacco shop in London.

The advertising mirror shown below is from the 1930s and probably hung in a tobacco shop, grocery, or drugstore where Black Cat cigarettes were sold. It measures 9″ x 15″. "Toast," owned by Fred and Dressel Tanenbaum, was caught in the act of looking for the Black Cat in the mirror. The die-cut lithographed sign at the right is from Canada and measures nearly four feet by four feet. When translated from the French, the cat is saying that Black Cats are the best-tasting cigarettes!

JOE'S CASINO

at the

BLACK CAT

JOE ENGLE, Manager

STATE ROAD, DELAWARE

PHONE: NEW CASTLE 303

After Prohibition ended in 1935, Joe's Casino at the Black Cat was a lively Delaware night spot that featured a huge dance hall, bar, and dining facilities. It was well known for its elaborate nightly floor shows and for attracting the best of the "big bands." The die-cut wine and drinks list shown at the left offered martinis for thirty-five cents and beer for fifteen cents! The facility also included the Black Cat cafeteria and tearoom. Plans for a Black Cat recreation park, complete with swimming pool, never materialized.

Black Cats have appeared on domestic cleaning supplies since the early days of this century. The Reit-Price Manufacturing Company dates back to 1900 and, according to corporate officials, the founders were in a conference room discussing company trademark possibilities when a large black cat jumped up on their table and inspired them! Today, a modernized black cat symbol (first used in 1954) appears on all the company's products. The dust mop shown below was discontinued in 1976 after approximately fifty years of production, but many other styles of Black Cat brand mops are still offered by the company. The celluloid advertising paperweight mirror is from the 1930s and shows the company's previous trademark.

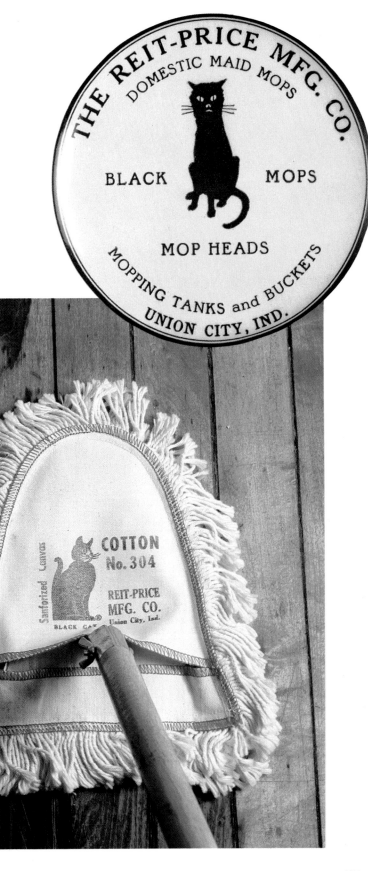

Before Prohibition, Black Cat Whiskey was produced by Ullman, Einstein & Co. of Cleveland, Ohio. This unusual brand was introduced in 1898, seventeen years after the company was founded, and the brand was considered so important that the cat figure even appeared on corporate stationery in the early 1900s. The company, like many others that sold alcoholic beverages, was dissolved in 1919, when liquor was outlawed by the 18th Amendment.

The black cat on the colorful Spanish advertising sign at the right is standing on a globe—as if to proclaim Black Cat Coffee the best brew in the world! The ornate embossed tin sign measures approximately 14″ x 19″ and is from around 1900.

Officials of The Nonsuch Mfg. Co. Limited of Toronto, Ontario, believed that "the black cat brings good luck" and even included that message in advertising for Black Cat Shoe Dressing. The brand was promoted with many kinds of advertising items given to customers, such as the billhook shown at the right and the wall-hanging kitchen match holder *(below)* from the early days of this century. The advertising clock on the opposite page was created for in-store advertising use probably before 1920, but the original ornate clock hands have been replaced with more modern ones. All pieces are lithographed tin; the clock has a wooden frame. The Nonsuch Co. was started in 1894, incorporated in 1897, and produced various kinds of polishes until dissolution in the 1960s.

Jacob Wellauer came to the United States from
Switzerland and started a small wholesale grocery
business in Milwaukee, Wisconsin, in 1863. By the 1880s,
when this tobacco crate label was printed, he could claim
over one million dollars in annual sales to retail grocers!
Like today, it was not unusual to find the seller's name
appearing on product labels. Sometimes the product
manufacturer would even organize "personalization" of
labels or signs for the individual dealers. Lithographers
who printed the labels and signs also offered this service.

60

This advertising poster was printed on inexpensive newsprint paper and could have been distributed as a handbill, pasted up on walls and fences or hung in a store window. It was used by Edward Kindred Elledge (born 1865), who operated a general store in Cincinnati, Iowa, from the 1890s through the 1930s. (The Elledge building still stands and carries the store name, but the store went out of business in the 1950s.) Since the Black Cat name was used on a number of different items carried in general stores over the years—such as tobacco, foods, and clothing—it's anyone's guess what the Black Cat product being advertised here actually was. Like so many companies from our country's past, the Henderson company that produced this Black Cat brand seems to have disappeared without a trace—except for this poster.

Over the years, black cats have appeared on all kinds of packaging associated with smoking. At the top left is a package of unusual dual-head matches bearing the Black Cat name in Spanish. They were produced in Mexico City in the 1920s.

The labels at the left are also from matchboxes. Black cats are favorite symbols around the world.

The Corbett Brothers Co. of New York City was known for fine silk and velvet ribbons identified by the Black Cat trademark. First registered in 1921, this symbol can be found on numerous promotional items created by the company throughout the years. Shown here are, from top to bottom, an advertising postcard mailed to a department store ribbon buyer announcing the arrival date of a Corbett Brothers sales representative; a folding celluloid measuring stick; a 1907 combination notepad and postage stamp holder that has a celluloid cover made to look like a small addressed postcard (front and back views); a folding celluloid pocket mirror; and a spool of Corbett Black Cat ribbon. Corbett Brothers' products were mostly used within the millinery industry. The company went out of business in the 1950s.

Charlie Black is the title of this painting by New York artist Susan Powers. Her work is known for exceptional color harmony, shadowing, and light reflection, especially noticeable on the whiskers and paws. This delightfully moody oil-on-canvas cat was created in 1982.

Black Cats at Home

s anyone who owns a cat (or is owned *by* a cat) will tell you—a house is not a home unless there's a feline around. And to most cat owners, the cat's color is not very important. It's the personality that counts. The intense friendships that blossom between pets and people transcend all color barriers.

But people who have shared their homes with many cats usually say the black ones are special—perhaps more loving, perhaps more mischievous, but always more vivid in the memories they leave behind.

The fascination with black cats around the house is immortalized by countless household objects bearing the black cat image. Some of the earliest examples are drawings and paintings of household pets dating back hundreds of years. In early American and Victorian times, cats of all colors were popular subjects and black cat designs as well as the others were stitched into embroidered samplers and onto quilts, painted onto china, stenciled onto wood, brushed onto canvas, formed into figurines, and sometimes even handcrafted out of metal into a weathervane to stand proudly atop a barn or house.

Today, around the world, most of the superstitions about black cats and bad luck have, at last, been discarded. Mail-order catalogs and department stores display black cats on towels, T-shirts, pajamas and nightshirts, tote bags and stationery, right along with all the other merchandise featuring various-colored felines. Cats are "in"—and black cats are no exception.

On the following pages you'll see some of our favorite examples of black cats—old and new—found around the house. It's only a fraction of the many kinds of things people have created through the years to feature black cats. But we think you'll agree that each is very special. Enhancing a design or stealing the show—these aren't just cats—they're *black cats!*

Black cats could make corresponding more interesting for people lucky enough to have these pencils and envelope seals among their desk accessories. The fuzzy pencil cats were first offered in the Department 56 company's line of giftware in 1985. The foil stickers were made for holiday use and sent season's greetings through the mail in the 1940s.

The works of Will Barnet, a popular contemporary artist, often feature members of his family and a sleek black cat. The cat is modeled after "Madame Butterfly," a beloved family pet for sixteen years. Although Madame Butterfly was a calico, Barnet exercised artistic license here to portray her as a black cat. *Cat and Canary* is a limited-edition lithograph commissioned by Associated American Artists in 1971. It commemorates the time Madame Butterfly was observed as she encountered the family's friendly, free-roaming canary. Knowing she should not harm it, the frustrated cat took a piece of paper from a wastebasket and ripped it apart with teeth and claws while watching the bird from afar! *Child Reading* is a limited-edition serigraph commissioned by the Westfield, New Jersey, Hadassah in 1970. The child is Barnet's daughter Ona when she was fifteen years old.

Whether displayed on a hearth or holding open a door, this painted black cat doorstop is a charming household decoration. The sleek design is typical of the Art Deco era. It stands 18" tall and is made of cast iron.

This decorative kitchen "egg box" was created in 1985 by Virginia artist Tavis Palmer. It is a beautiful likeness of "Licorice," a pet cat belonging to Karol Atkinson of Mercer, Pennsylvania. Palmer is a versatile artist, particularly recognized for her realistic paintings of children and pets. Her works include fashion illustration, advertising, and greeting card art, but the New Jersey native prefers capturing nature on canvas in her rustic barn studio in the Shenandoah Valley.

"Lucy Goosey's Pet Cat" is an updated gooseneck lamp for the cat lover of the 1980s. Introduced by Kovac's Design Group in 1983, the cat's face is painted glazed ceramic. In addition to the table lamp, it is also available as a floor lamp or clip-on extension lamp in white as well as black.

And, if you believe good things come in small packages, you'll love the Hallmark black cat–handle box. Hallmark is well known for its line of greeting cards, dating back to 1910, when the company was called Hall Brothers, Inc. The name changed in 1954 and today the company has products as diversified as specialty jewelry, posters, plush toys, and art supplies. The black cat design was introduced in 1984.

There's nothing like having a cat around for comfort when you're not feeling well. So you can just imagine how many people feeling under the weather have perked up when they received the adorable get-well greeting card above! Titled "Feel Better Soon," it was created by Los Angeles illustrator Bob Hickson in 1981 and offered by Paper Moon Graphics, Inc.

Volume 14

$4.00

Number 3

THE ARMCHAIR DETECTIVE

The *Black Cat Detective Series* makes entertaining reading even today, some forty years after the Crestwood Publishing Co. printed the twenty-eight-book series. The cat logo is found on the front and back of each of the digest-sized paperback novels. During the same time period, the black cat also catered to readers who loved cowboys and the Wild West with the twelve-book *Black Cat Western Series.* The inset shows a plastic-coated advertising pocket mirror given away during the 1940s.

Mystery lovers expect to find black cats prowling through the stories they read. But surprisingly, there aren't as many as you might think! At the left is an illustration by Stanley Woods of Dr. Nikola and his constant companion, Apollyon. They are characters in turn-of-the-century detective novels by Australian novelist Guy Boothby. In one story, crime solver Dr. Nikola says, "Apollyon and I are not unlike. When we get out our claws, we are dangerous." The illustration originally appeared on the cover of the novel *Farewell Nikola* in 1901 and made a beautiful cover for *The Armchair Detective* magazine in 1981.

ISSN: 0710-2844   Vol.1 No.4   WINTER 1981/1982   Price $2.50

BLACK CAT

MYSTERY QUARTERLY

*Tales of Crime, Detection
and the Supernatural
Serials, Puzzles and Games*

The *Black Cat* mystery magazine was produced in Canada during the 1980s. Its stories ranged from the eerie to general detective fiction. Although it could be found in England, Germany, and the United States as well as Canada, it did not have wide distribution and is no longer published. Although the name is the same as *The Black Cat* magazine shown on the facing page, there was no connection between the two publications.

The Black Cat magazine was a Victorian monthly featuring short fiction stories penned entirely by amateur writers. To obtain the rights to the stories, the publisher, Herman D. Umbstaetter, advertised his writing contests in other popular magazines, and awarded cash prizes for winning entries. The stories often had unusual plot twists, giving the magazine a reputation for the unexpected. In the magazine's early years, each cover displayed a full-figural black cat, usually dressed in a colorful costume. Umbstaetter's wife, Nelly Littlehale Umbstaetter, drew the charming covers beginning with the first issue in October 1895. By 1898, covers had been changed to show only the cat's face, surrounded by various figural, floral, or geometric designs. The last issue appeared in 1923.

The Black Cat

5 CENTS

June 1897.

THE SHORTSTORY PUBLISHING CO., 144 HIGH ST. BOSTON, MASS.

Cats were sometimes the favorite subjects of popular music around the turn of the century. Families could spend hours gathered around the parlor piano to sing and play tunes in the days before radio and television entertainment were available. The words of "The Cat's Whiskers" describe an aging cat that has been left by her tom for a younger kitty. This 1923 story of a lost love could have been—and perhaps was—meant to portray the pain of a jilted girl friend. In the song, the older cat's whiskers have turned gray—just as they are in the illustration. *"Das Kater-Lied"* was published in Germany in 1910. The title means "The Cat Song" from *Alma, Where Do You Live?,* a Parisian vaudeville show. "The Cats' Parade," published in 1900, was a tribute by the composer to some friends who were disturbed at night by "neighbors' cats holding midnight parties" in their yards. There are no words but "meows" occasionally appear in the music.

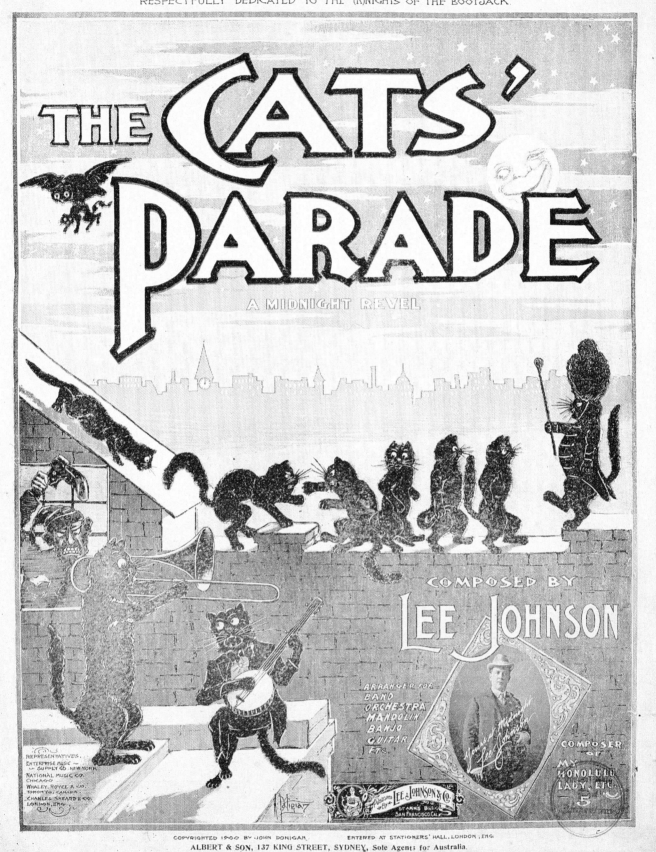

Sometimes comedy revues or plays from the early twentieth century included songs or routines about cats. But this 1918 British music sheet cover only uses the stylized black cat as an attention-getting device. The song is not about a cat at all!

In the early years of this century, when postcards were the most popular form of correspondence, some particularly interesting cats appeared on cards made by foreign publishers. The fuzzy texture of the cats and other artistic touches on the cards shown above create a three-dimensional effect. The card with the chimney-sitting cat has both a French and German advertising message on the reverse side for ERA margarine. The cat's head is a separate piece and can move left and right. The standing cat is from Germany and has inset amber-colored glass eyes. The German holiday cat card has an easel attached to the back of the cutout cat figure so the card can lie flat and the cat with a jeweled eye can sit upright. The smiling French cat face has gold-colored celluloid eyes and a pink celluloid mouth. All are circa 1920.

This limited-edition porcelain figure of the Egyptian cat goddess Bastet was made as a replica of the original Egyptian statue by The Boehm Studio. It was part of the second Boehm collection of Egyptian antiquities made in conjunction with the "Treasures of Tutankhamun" exhibit sent from the Cairo Museum and displayed at U.S. museums from 1976 through 1979. The figure measures 10¼″ high x 6½″ deep and is exceptionally detailed, with rich colors and accents of pure gold. It was made in 1978 and is number 351 of 1,000.

Black cats have been guarding French vineyards, orchards, and gardens since 1937. Hanging from branches, the unusual metal cat faces have reflective eyes that catch the light in much the same way a real cat's eyes would. Birds, mice, and other predators are frightened away as they are tricked into believing a live cat is patrolling the area! Over 20 million of these silent "watchcats" have been sold in France. They were introduced to the American market in 1970 by The Yeoman Group.

This unusual cat looks like an antique but it is really a modern creation. Surrounded by peacock feathers, the cat doll wears a Victorian-style dress with lace trim. It can be used as a beautiful holiday tree ornament or as a door decoration to take the place of the more traditional evergreen wreath. In Ireland, where cats have long represented good luck, cat ornaments are often hung on doors to bring luck to the household. This special cat was offered in 1985 by Flights of Fancy of New York City.

One of the most charming party goods designs of the 1980s is "Fat Cat" by Mark Havers. The Haut Papier company, founded by entrepreneur John R. Ross in 1979, introduced this adorably pudgy cat in its 1980 line. One later variation replaced the cat's bandana with a green holiday wreath for seasonal parties. Luckily for those who appreciate pleasingly plump pussycats, the colorful plastic glasses and cocktail napkins are still available in the Haut Papier line.

he toy world changes constantly. Like art, literature, and advertising, it reflects the fashions, social values, and fads of the times. In this strange land, cartoon characters and comic book heroes come to life, and can sometimes take the place of playmates on a rainy afternoon.

But even in today's high-tech toy world, there are countless children who would rather spend at least some of their afternoons playing with their pets. And, through the years, the makers of toys and games have always acknowledged the fascination children have with animals by including cat, dog, and other animal themes on the many different kinds of pastimes they offer.

Children can be pretty energetic as they play—so the toys and games shown are "survivors" from yesteryear. They've survived both the children who played with them and the adults who eventually threw away almost everything from childhood that was not considered a necessity for living in the world of grownups!

These black cats delight all who are lucky enough to find them today. It's easy to see why they were saved.

Christmas Wishes

This holiday card (enlarged), postmarked 1913, shows the natural friendship and sharing between children and cats, a scene created virtually every day around the world.

Perhaps the most realistic of all plush toy black cats are Steiff cats, easily identified by a "button in the ear" that holds the famous company's label. Margarete Steiff, a German seamstress, first started sewing toy animals in 1880. Demand rapidly grew, and today the Margarete Steiff company, which is renowned for first developing the Teddy Bear, features over 600 toys in its line. The Steiff black cats were made from the 1920s to the 1980s. *Back row, left to right:* ca. 1920, 1950, 1979. *Front row:* 1967, 1980, 1983.

This delightful windup cat must have amused adults as well as children throughout the years. When wound with the key, this mechanical kitten scoots along chasing its ball on tiny wheels, then rolls itself completely over before moving along again. It is 5″ long and has plushy cotton/rayon "fur." A more stereotyped black cat scene is found on the cover of the Skit Skat game below. Made by the American Toy Works of New York, the game has brilliant Art Deco colors and several cardboard cat cutouts inside. American Toy Works went out of business in 1954.

Right: Victorian parlor games featured some charming black cats. In the Black Cat Fortune Telling Game, first introduced by Parker Brothers in 1897, players could "tell the past, present and future" by drawing cards randomly and lining up the phrases printed on the backs to form complete sentences. The Black Cat Dominoes box, also from Parker Brothers, held a set of standard dominoes (no cats were pictured on them), but the box lid was dressed up with the colorfully clothed black cat illustration. Both games are from before 1901. The cute cat "spinner" is from a children's board game from about the same time period.

Mariah is the name of this endearing modern-day cat, painted in the
primitive folk art style of the early nineteenth century. Evergreen
Press, Inc. included the image in a line of greeting cards introduced in
1983. The painting was originally part of the Shell River Collection of
American Folk Art, Birmingham, Alabama.

The smiling cats at the left are "Shadow Cats," huggable fabric-
covered toys available in 1987 from Overly-Raker, Inc. The
company has been making plush animals since 1976 and, in
addition to "Shadow Cats," makes yellow "Sunshine Kitties."

The Lucky Black Cat

Louis Wain may have done more to promote the image of black cats than any other artist of the early 1900s. Wain drew these cats as part of several series of cat postcards with the "good luck" theme. Mostly remembered as an artist of the comical dressed-up animals popular in Victorian times, Wain illustrated many books and his art is found in late Victorian advertising and lithographed prints, as well as postcards. Supposedly, he first became interested in cats when he adopted a kitten. He was so captivated by the little animal that he began drawing cats profusely and soon became a self-proclaimed cat "authority" whose writings, as well as art, were highly in demand.

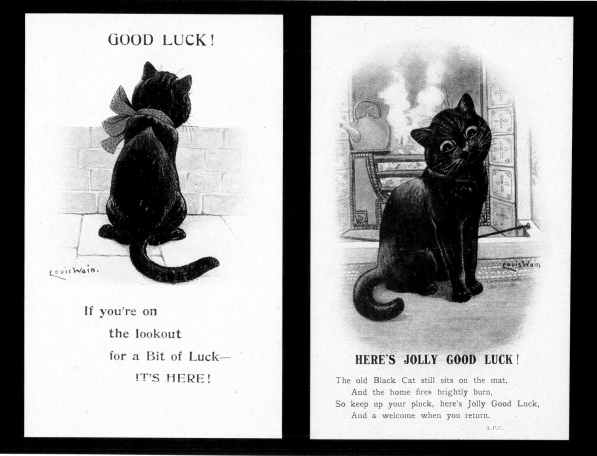

GOOD LUCK!

If you're on
the lookout
for a Bit of Luck—
IT'S HERE!

HERE'S JOLLY GOOD LUCK!

The old Black Cat still sits on the mat,
And the home fires brightly burn,
So keep up your pluck, here's Jolly Good Luck,
And a welcome when you return.

A.P.C.

Look closely at these four dressed-up cats and you'll discover that while they all look very much alike each face is decidedly different. The original designs by British artist Sue Boettcher were commissioned by Department 56, an American specialty giftware company. Both plates and mugs are made of fine porcelain and are imported from Japan. They were first available in 1985.

Hooked rugs are increasingly being recognized as important pieces of folk art. This 33″ x 17¾″ wool rug is an early twentieth-century example that combines bright, colorful accents with a traditional animal motif. Rugs, like paintings and tapestries, generally reflect subjects of importance to the artist, but there's no way to tell if a trio of playful black cats posed for the design below or if the rug was simply woven from a printed pattern.

A most unusual piece of handmade folk art, this charming cat chair was created by a skilled craftsman for a very special child. The smiling cats are painted on both sides, and the back measures 26″ high. Jill Rosenberg of Chicago, Illinois, looks completely at home nestled between the cats, much as a child of the 1920s must have looked when the chair was new.

The International Order of Hoo-Hoo has a long association with the black cat. The purpose of this fraternal organization, founded in 1892 as the "Concatonated" (United) Order of Hoo-Hoo, is to promote the lumber and forest products industry. The black cat was adopted as the group's symbol to represent the unconventional nature of the organization and was considered an antisuperstition good-luck sign.

Over the years, members have been encouraged to use the cat in promoting their own businesses—so it's not unusual to see the cat on premiums like the red-and-white celluloid tape measure case from a St. Louis lumber firm or to find the cat appearing on corporate checks such as those shown from around the turn of the century made for a Texas firm. There was even a special Hoo-Hoo song in 1904, and a tobacco brand was named Hoo-Hoo in the group's honor.

The society points out that the cat's tail is curved in the shape of a numeral 9—the official Hoo-Hoo lucky number. Every September (the ninth month), the group's annual convention is held. Several convention badges are shown here —the colorful pinback button was from the 1899 Denver convention and the ornate metal badge was from the Chicago gathering in 1908. Today, the society has over 8,000 members in 129 chapters worldwide.

Bright-eyed, playful, and ready to please is "Winklebean," a pet adopted by Michael Querry and Lisa Prado from Chicago's Tree House Animal Foundation. Humane workers say black cats still encounter a certain amount of discrimination in the world, and many arrive every year at pet adoption centers because some people don't want a black cat around the house. Luckily, this negative perception is changing and, along with every other kind of cat, black cats are now regularly finding good loving homes as cats become the most popular pet in America.

One of the most interesting black cats is found on this poster stamp (enlarged). Advertisers produced "miniature posters" to promote products as early as the 1840s, but the popularity of using such stamps for advertising grew rapidly only when improved printing processes of the late 1800s and early 1900s made high-quality color reproduction available. Although poster stamps could not be used to mail letters, they were collected by the public in the early decades of this century and kept in albums much as advertising trade cards were saved by the Victorians. Collecting of poster stamps had peaked by the 1940s, but many nice examples were saved and are still enjoyed today.

Acknowledgments

We would like to thank the people who helped us in the creation of *The Black Cat Made Me Buy It!*

Brandt Aymar, editor at Crown Publishers, Inc., for his continued enthusiasm and support; *Jane Jordan Browne,* for representing us; and *Ken Kapson,* for again sharing his knowledge of history and antiques with us.

In addition, a number of items shown in this book were made available for photography by collectors and antiques dealers. Our most sincere appreciation to *Karol Atkinson* for allowing us to include items shown on pages 2, 10, 11, 14, 15-bottom, 16-bottom, 19, 20, 39, 45, 59, 60, 69, 86-top, 92, and 93. *Jackie Geyer* for items on pages 15-top, 41-bottom, 51-bottom, 53, 55-bottom, 57, and 70-right. *Myron Huffman,* page 5 and back cover-bottom right. *Dave and Phylliss Harris,* page 21. *Sandy* and *John Millns,* pages 3 and 90. *Susan Nicholson,* page 79. We also would like to thank the following companies for their help in making items available to us: *Jockey International, Inc.,* page 43; *Julius Kayser & Co.,* division of The Seagram Classics Wine Company, page 48; *The Catnip Shoppé,* pages 81 and 82; *Overly-Raker, Inc.,* pages 2 and 88.

Photo Credits: All photography in *The Black Cat Made Me Buy It!* is the work and creativity of *Peter Basdeka,* except those photos by: *Barry M. Sawyer,* pp. 5 and back cover-bottom right, and 21; *Joe Renckly,* pp. 15-top, 41-bottom, 51-bottom, 53, and 57. Photo on p. 65 courtesy of *Jay Johnson, Inc.;* photo on p. 85 courtesy of *Margarete Steiff GmbH;* photo on p. 95 copyright 1986 *Donna Coss, C.P.P.,* all rights reserved.

We also appreciate the cooperation of the many companies that gave us permission to reproduce their advertising or products: COVER AND TITLE PAGE ILLUSTRATION: Julius Kayser and Zeller Schwarze Katz label are trademarks of Julius Kayser & Co. Used by permission of The Seagram Classics Wine Company, exclusive U.S. importer. (4-top) The renowned Black Cat® trademark for firecrackers is registered in the United States Patent and Trademark Office and is owned by Li & Fung (Trading) Ltd., Hong Kong. Reprinted by permission. (4-bottom) Copyright 1977, Taylor & Ng. (6-left) Courtesy of Dorene Publishing Co., Inc., Arlington, Tx. (12) Copyright 1985, Carlton Cards, Inc. (28-30) Cat's Paw name and logos are trademarks of The Biltrite Corporation, Waltham, Ma. (46-left) Leonard Kreusch Zeller Schwarze Katz QBA. (46-right-48) Julius Kayser and Zeller Schwarze Katz label are trademarks of Julius Kayser & Co. Used by permission of The Seagram Classics Wine Company, exclusive U.S. importer. (64) Copyright 1982, Susan Powers. *Charlie Black,* oil on canvas, courtesy of Jay Johnson America's Folk Heritage Gallery, New York City. (65) "Black Cat" pencils are a Sue Boettcher design, United Kingdom, Copyright Department 56, U.S.A. (66) Copyright 1971, Will Barnet. (67) Copyright 1970, Will Barnet. (69) Copyright 1985, Tavis Palmer. (70-right) Copyright 1984, Hallmark Cards. Used with permission. (72) Reprinted permission of *The Armchair Detective,* 129 W. 56th St., N.Y., N.Y. 10019. (76) © 1951, Ched Music Corp., P.O. Box 221, New York, NY 10021. (80) Courtesy of The Yeoman Group. (82) Used by permission of R. Palen and Flights of Fancy, New York, N.Y. (83) Copyright 1980, Haut Papier, Inc. (85) Courtesy Margarete Steiff GmbH. (87-left) The Black Cat Fortune Telling Game and Black Cat Dominoes game used with permission from Parker Brothers. (88) Used by permission of Overly-Raker, Inc. (89) Copyright 1983, Evergreen Press, Inc. (91) "Cat's Meow" plates and mugs are a Sue Boettcher design, United Kingdom, copyright Department 56, U.S.A.

Every effort has been made to contact the copyright and trademark owners or their representatives. If there have been any omissions, please notify the publisher for inclusion in future printings.